A Trainer's Guide to Performing a Systems Training Needs Analysis

Your no B.S. Guide to Creating a Full TNA with Facts, Evidence and Recommendations

Tom Mcguire

All rights reserved. No part of this book may be reproduced or distributed in any form without prior written permission from the author, with the exception of non-commercial uses permitted by copyright law.

No part of this book may be reproduced or transmitted by any means, except as permitted by UK copyright law or the author. For licensing requests, please contact the author at me@email.co.uk.

All rights reserved. No portion of this book may be reproduced, copied, distributed or adapted in any way, with the exception of certain activities permitted by applicable copyright laws, such as brief quotations in the context of a review or academic work. For permission to publish, distribute or otherwise reproduce this work, please contact the author at torrit@me.com.

Edition 1

Copyright © 2022 Tom Mcguire

All rights reserved.

ISBN:9798832330167

This book is dedicated to my wife Victoria Mcguire. Her love, support and encouragement in creating this book have been essential.

I'd also like to thank Cherry Anderson, Irina McBain, Paul Dollah, Simon Glass, Jamie Boyle, Raza Siddiqui, Ash Halim, Anthony Hargreaves, Scott Smith, Ellis Stewart, Khayyam Rehman, Steve Stimson, Helen Baldwin, Karl Jones, Lee Thompson, Jacci Wright, Andy Brook, Ruth Williams, Phil Puddefoot, Tom Sewell, Matt Okesola, Dr Anthony Cairns, Andrew Shipley, Ralph Tuckwell, Paul Nichols, Will James and Michael Rogan.

CONTENTS

PROLOGUE: Why is it Important to do a TNA (training needs analysis)? ... 1

Chapter 1 - What is a Training Needs Analysis? ... 7

    What is a Training Needs Analysis (TNA)? ... 7

    Avoiding Mistakes and Taking Opportunities ... 11

    Return on Investment ... 13

    Making Recommendations ... 15

Chapter 2 - First Things First ... 18

    First Things First ... 18

    Ten Key Steps to Completing your TNA ... 21

    Interview the Sponsor ... 22

    Why, What and How ... 27

Chapter 3 - Use a Successful Method ... 30

    Use a Successful Method ... 30

    The Main TNA Document ... 32

Chapter 4 - Interview with a Business Analyst ... 42

    Interview with a Business Analyst ... 42

    The right words make all the difference ... 45

    The Interview ... 48

Chapter 5 - Interview with a Change Manager ... 51

Interview with a Change Manager ... 51

The Interview ... 53

The Change Impact Analysis Document ... 57

Chapter 6 - Interview with a Test Manager and a Team Manager ... 60

Test Manager ... 60

Team Manager ... 64

Chapter 7 - How to Transform the Taxonomy into Courses ... 68

Taxonomy ... 68

Score 1 and Score 2 ... 72

Additional Tasks and Courses ... 75

Chapter 8 - Courses, Roles and Delegates ... 79

Roles Matrix ... 79

Delegates ... 82

Excel Skills ... 83

Chapter 9 - How to Summarise Your Findings ... 86

Events So Far ... 86

Editing the Main TNA Document ... 90

Chapter 10 - What do People Really Think ABout TNAs? ... 95

Tom Sewell ... 95

Matt Okesola	99
Dr Anthony Cairns	101
Andrew Shipley	103
Chapter 11 - How to Present Your TNA	107
How to present your TNA	107
Epilogue	117

Prologue

Why is it Important to do a TNA (training needs analysis)?

"Making assumptions simply means believing things are a certain way with little or no evidence that shows you are correct, and you can see at once how this can lead to terrible trouble." - Lemony Snicket, 'The Austere Academy'

You may wonder why this is a trainer's guide. When I was 23, I was working for a large international IT Company in the UK as a salesperson. It was a terrific experience, but I knew I wanted more. I applied for a re-training scheme, to be trained for a technical role. Fortunately, I was selected by the technical training team. A year later and I was teaching programming and systems administration. People saw my potential as a trainer and gave me a great opportunity just when I needed it. I am still a trainer now and I love it. I want to give my experience to others in a practical, no nonsense way. Whether you are an employee or a freelancer, this book will help you build a robust TNA that will rock!

I've now been a freelance training consultant for over 20 years. Through experience, I've learned that a good TNA can save you time and heartache on a training project. I have worked on several projects where the TNA was 'lite'. This made it difficult to know where to start and what to focus on and what was out of scope. There have been situations where I have created material and then found out that it was no longer required. To be cynical, as a freelancer I could have just focused on billing my time and not worried about it, but I am proud of my work and I like to see it used.

What can be achieved with an effective TNA? We provide facts, evidence, and recommendations. The facts are a summary of your findings, such as the number of people and what they need to learn. The evidence is the data you have collected, which you will need to support your facts when challenged. Your ideas on how to design, build and deliver the training are the recommendations. I've found it useful to provide one set of facts and three suggestions. People love choice and will always prefer that than a single rigid outcome.

In the real world, you need to be aware of costs too. Your three suggestions need to have timings and costs so the client can evaluate those aspects. You can label them in anyway that you find resonates with the organisation. I've seen the "Good, Better and Best" method used to label the suggestions, but I think this puts the client in a position where they feel "Bad" about selecting the "Good" option. Personally, I prefer to group my recommendations around the delivery methods, such as "Classroom, Blended, E-Learning".

You may be an employee in an organisation and know how to pitch the TNA perfectly. Alternatively, you may be a freelancer and your assignment is to produce the TNA and then leave. In either situation, I've found it essential to explain the method you are using to produce the TNA with the person who's going to sign it off. This shows that you know what you're doing. You have a great opportunity here to raise standards for the client and they will appreciate it.

I was once hired to do a TNA for a financial software implementation. A TNA had been delivered previously, but it had failed. The users were working on the live system. A court case was in process over a disputed supplier invoice for several million pounds. The payments manager placed a hold on the supplier so that the invoice would not be paid until they had settled the court case. Unfortunately, the hold was placed at the wrong level and the invoice was paid mistakenly the following month. The client abandoned the court case and had to pay the costs for both sides.

I did the second TNA and recommended 42 days of training development and 11 days of classroom training, plus some instant 'hot topic' sessions to be delivered immediately. I ended up working with that client for eight months. I gave them a training catalogue for existing colleagues and new recruits. Everybody knew what training they needed for each job role. There were no further multi-million pound errors.

I will include some strategies in this book for interviewing people in specific job roles who you will need to meet. These individuals provide resources for you and will save you a great deal of time. The questions are different depending on each job role and I recommend you use the templates I supply on www.trainersguide.guru to record the responses.

I use the word "organisation" throughout this book. You may be in a government department, a software company or a paper mill. It doesn't matter as the principles in the book will serve you well.

The focus is on a "Systems" TNA. This is different from other books which deal with behavioural change. A behavioural TNA attempts to identify gaps where training can improve performance. A systems TNA is designed to prepare the people in the organisation to use the new system. You will be unlikely to go down to the level of the individual or even to a specific team within a group. Your focus will be on the organisation roles that the system supports. Everybody in the organisation must fit into one or more roles. If you know the roles and the role membership, you have the key to targeting the training successfully.

Typically, a new system in an organisation will provide new ways of carrying out existing tasks. These new methods should be quicker and cheaper, but essentially the inputs and the outputs are the same. Bold organisations go beyond this and I recommend you keep this in mind. How big is the change and what can you do to ensure the training need is fully met?

I hope you enjoy the book and that you find it useful. I'd love you to contact me and let me know how it has made a difference to you and your organisation (Torrit@me.com).

Cheers
Tom Mcguire

Chapter 1

What is a Training Needs Analysis (TNA)?

"Learning is not attained by chance, it must be sought for with ardor and attended to with diligence." - Abigail Adams

Organisations live in a fast-changing world. Whether it's a sales-driven company or a government department doesn't matter: the products and services have to change to stay ahead. I worked with a large telecoms client which spent £100 million on a new human resources system. Five years later, I was called back to work on another 'new' human resources system. I asked what had happened to the 'old' one, and apparently it had been excellent but no longer did what was required. All of that work and effort from five years ago was now going to be switched off. These triggers for change are happening of all the time.

The effort of implementing a new system only has one purpose, which is to solve a problem, such as:

- A forced software upgrade
- New legislation meaning a system change
- Company merger
- Automation of a manual process

Evidence

A TNA is an evidence document. Your organisation will use this to apply a budget, book developers, trainers, software, classrooms, documentation and the time of the delegates. This is an enormous investment and deserves serious consideration. I would love to think that training is the highest priority in a project, but sadly, this is unlikely to be true. You need to have a straightforward way of gathering your information and resources.

Data is powerful and cannot be resisted. If you have accurate data, then you can perform a useful what-if analysis in Excel to try out different scenarios. The core data we need in a TNA is:

- Roles
- Course descriptions
- Course durations
- Numbers of trainers
- Numbers of delegates
- Locations
- Costs
- Timing

You should keep in mind the bigger aim behind the work that you're doing and let this guide you. Organisations love problem solvers. Once they know what is needed, they can plan around the cost and the time required and reduce the risk of failure.

A TNA is an opportunity to take a snapshot of where the organisation and its people are. What skills do they have right now and what do they need to meet the challenge of the coming change? A good TNA identifies the gaps at role level. It is an unnecessary luxury to go beyond this and tailor training plans to the individual level. The organisation should guide you to what level is required.

The TNA document must provide solid evidence to back up all of your recommendations. I've presented several TNAs at board meetings. Directors at board level will often pick one aspect of a proposal and then drill down through it. These people are busy and they need to know that you can defend every aspect of your TNA. This can be stressful, so you have to make sure you can justify all of your findings. If you follow the method I suggest, you will have the following documents:

- Main TNA.docx - a Word document covering all the important findings
- Main TNA.ppt - a PowerPoint presentation with summaries and recommendations
- TNA Workbook.xlsx - an Excel spreadsheet with multiple worksheets containing detailed data to generate the summaries

Action Step - I have created templates for these and other documents you will need. You can download them from www.trainersguide.guru

You must be able to prove every element in your TNA. Your sponsor at board level is going to back your proposal, but the other directors may have their own reasons for objecting to it. You need to be rock solid with your facts and your sponsor will thank you for it. I have seen people knocked back in meetings like this and with some careful preparation you can avoid this happening to you.

Avoiding Mistakes and Taking Opportunities

I believe it is also possible to help the organisation avoid mistakes and to take opportunities. This is great for adding value and building your reputation.

I have seen many training mishaps over the years that a good quality TNA could have avoided and here are a few:

- Forgetting about the 120 employees in another country with another language. This is a tough situation to turn around quickly.

- Designing video-based learning but failing to allow for streaming not working on the network for 50% of the locations. It's complicated to provide a different technical solution at this stage.
- Training was created for 2,000 people in a call centre, but no one told the Planning Managers and they refused to take their staff off the phones for training. They suggested a wait of three months so they could plan it in. Timings and communication are key to avoid a situation like this one.
- 75 people were trained to respond to calls about a new product, but only five took the calls. This meant 70 people wasted their time attending the training.
- All human resource teams were trained on managing maternity leave, but only two people were responsible for it. It is easy to make assumptions about processes and roles, so you must ask the right questions.

There are opportunities too. It is your responsibility to challenge the organisation and raise standards. I will cover this later when I talk about adding extras, but here are a few suggestions:

- Moving to an E-Learning solution so people can plan their own time for training.
- Introducing online tests to confirm the training has been effective.
- Integrating your training into the organisation skills matrix so that it is recognised as an essential role based skill.
- Providing opportunities for colleagues to become super-users.
- Using training material to drive the production of standard operating procedures.
- Doing a reconciliation between test scripts and business processes.

Return on Investment

Most organisations I've worked with are keen to prove they have spent their money well. You could estimate how much an error costs the company and train the users to reduce those mistakes. Costs saved minus the training costs should give you a positive outcome. Estimating the cost of errors is a hard task and I'd suggest you ask the organisation to do it and provide you with the information.

Another way of looking at this is to train colleagues to save money for the organisation. A good example is when I worked at a large supermarket in the UK. It implemented a new solution for scanning incoming invoices from suppliers. The system worked, but the hit rate on producing a perfect invoice from a scan was below 50%. I trained the users to work with the suppliers to change their invoices, which improved the hit rate to 80%. This saved a great deal of time and the suppliers were paid on time more frequently.

Asking the Right Questions

As a keen amateur photographer, I used to be asked by friends and family to do wedding photographs. It was probably the most stressful thing I've ever done, but also great fun. I made mistakes at the beginning, such as missing favourite uncles or children from previous partners in the pictures. The bride and groom never mentioned these people

Key Chapter One Takeaways

- A good TNA identifies gaps at multiple levels.
    - Understand how far you need to drill down.
- You must have evidence and facts to back up your recommendations.
    - You will be badly burnt at board level if you are vague about details.
- Challenge the organisation to raise standards.
    - They might say no, but they will respect you for pushing them.
- Avoid mistakes.
    - Ask 'stupid questions'. You can't afford to miss anything.
- Make multiple recommendations.
    - Give the organisation choices. This will make you standout as a consultant rather than just a trainer and it will increase their buy-in.
- Do nothing other than the TNA.
    - There will be no overtime pay! Stop at the TNA and then build the training plan as a separate task.

Chapter 2

First Things First

"Everyone in a complex system has a slightly different interpretation. The more interpretations we gather, the easier it becomes to gain a sense of the whole." - Margaret J. Wheatley.

If you are an established employee in an organisation, you will have a good feel for the structure and the personalities involved in a project. I wrote this chapter from the perspective of a person who has just joined. You may find that some of the work has already been done and you can use it to create your TNA. I would also recommend that you approach the process with an open mind. We can all bring our previous experience to a TNA, but this can sometimes prejudice the outcome.

Action Step - Ask the training function in the organisation if they have a standard way of doing TNAs and if so, can they share it with you.

I once worked with a large manufacturing company which had already started a TNA. However, this had become large and unwieldy, it was going nowhere and the person who created it had lost their way. The level of detail was immense, but very little attention had been paid to the key questions. Instead, the designer of the TNA had focused on creating a spreadsheet covering the functionality of the new software system. They hadn't asked which functions were going to be used by who and if there were any incremental phases to this rollout plan. They made assumptions about existing skills and knowledge and instead focused on designing training material before the TNA had been signed off. The spreadsheet became a special object that the employee had to control. This was when I was called in to help. The first thing I did was state that I needed to start at the beginning and the spreadsheet had to go. It's amazing how the spreadsheet was so highly valued until someone identified its real value. The client breathed a sigh of relief. No more battles over spreadsheets. The TNA could now begin for real. I also agreed with the sponsor that I would focus on the TNA only.

Top Tip - Do not stray from the TNA. Do not get involved in the following:
- Designing the training
- Developing training materials
- Coaching staff 1 to 1 or delivering training
- Solving people's problems with the current system

Learning and Development Team

You should reach out to the Learning and Development team in the organisation. This could be 20 people or nobody at all. It amazed me when working with a multi billion dollar turnover manufacturer that they had no learning and development (L&D) team. They had a health and safety training manager, but nothing else. As a contrast, I worked with a financial services company with an L&D team of 20. Every single training document had to be reviewed by the training manager and then reviewed again by the legal team. Investigate the local L&D culture and ask the following:

- What are the corporate standards for TNAs?
- Do the findings of the TNA need to fit into a bigger training plan?

Ten Key Steps to Completing your TNA

1. Understand the overall requirement
2. Create your own templates for recording your findings
3. Get an introduction from your sponsor to the organisation and project team
4. Appoint a review team of recognised leaders
5. Ask the questions and record the answers
6. Use the templates to record your data:
    - Courses
    - Delegates
    - Events
    - Trainers
7. Have the TNA reviewed

8. Summarise your findings
9. Have the TNA reviewed again
10. Present your TNA

Interview the Sponsor

It is essential that you interview your sponsor very early on. This is the person on the project who will sign off the TNA. Typically, they will have chosen you to do the TNA, so should be on your side. You need to find out from this person what the aim of the TNA is and what the scope is. It is very easy (especially if you are a subject expert) to assume you know exactly what is required and dive straight in.

I have seen this happen with a large pharmaceutical company where the training offered was just too technical. The delegates were left floundering, felt stressed and had no backup. Have a meeting with the sponsor and get them to explain the overall aim of the training. This is not the TNA itself, this is understanding the overall picture.

Key questions you should ask at this meeting:

- What is the overall aim of the TNA?
- Who needs training?
- What do they need to do after the training?
- Is this part of a bigger project that could affect the training?
- When is the training needed?
- What will happen if they do not complete the training?

That last question seems like an odd one, but I really like it. It places the question in the sponsor's mind and may strengthen their resolve to support you. I would immediately follow up with a request that they communicate to the organisation that you are starting the TNA and to expect to get involved. This instruction from the sponsor gives you the authority to reach out to people and expect a response.

Top Tip - Document every meeting you have with people. If it is a Zoom/Teams call, then ask for permission to record it. If you are meeting face to face or on the phone, have a form available that you can fill in. You will meet lots of people and have lots of discussions. If you don't document them, you will get confused, and the response becomes unusable. You do not want to go back to someone to ask the same questions again.

Download the sponsor_interview.docx document from www.trainersguide.guru

Who's who?

Always ask for an organisation chart of the people working on the project. Typically, in a systems implementation, this will be a mixture of project only people and employees. You need to find out who these people are, as they are a major source of information for you. Reach out to the leads in the following roles:

- Project manager
    - Request a meeting to get an overview of the project and the timelines
- Subject matter expert (SME)
    - Ask for the business background to how the processes work
- Environment manager

- Request access to the test and training systems
- Testing manager
  - Ask if there are any test scripts available and if can you have access to the script repository
- Business analyst
  - Request a copy of all the business processes and lower-level documents
- Change manager
  - Ask for a copy of the change impact analysis document
- Comms manager
  - Ask for the comms plan

Imagine if we lived in a perfect world where the following was true:

- Everything was planned and well executed
- People responded to emails
- Everybody attended meetings when invited
- Documentation was rich and accurate

The bad news is that we don't live in a perfect world. Our imperfect world often presents us with the following:

- Slipped project dates
- People leaving the project
- Implementation partners being replaced
- Delays to the rollout

You need to start early in building your relationships and be prepared to invest some time in them. In reality, you are asking for everything from these people and not giving anything back until the TNA is finished. A friend of mine used to find out what people liked to drink from the canteen and invited them to meetings there with the promise of hot chocolate or coffees on him. It worked, although it was a tad expensive. The point is that you need to be comfortable with introducing yourself and expressing what you need clearly.

Action Step - Get a copy of the organisation chart for the project or create your own.

Review Team

Another essential is to ask the sponsor to identify a review team. These are respected people who have an excellent knowledge of the business and the project. I recommend you set up a team of three reviewers. One person isn't enough, as you need more than one opinion. If you have over three, then you can have too many.

The role of the reviewers is to check your findings regularly. I would ask them to commit to this and be part of the sign-off. They should provide a sanity check but also give you suggestions about things that you may have missed or incorrectly included.

Why, What and How

Whenever I create a document, I like to keep in mind these three key words. Everybody absorbs and understands information in different ways.

Why

This is the comprehensive overview at the beginning explaining why you are doing the TNA. The questions that you asked the sponsor at the very beginning will inform this section. Do you remember the last question for the sponsor? "What will happen if the training is not completed?". This might sound like a negative question, but it goes to the heart of the matter. You need to get the answer and include it and use it to promote action and engagement.

What

Here you have the meat of the TNA. The details about how many people, what roles, what skills and the gap between the current and desired state.

How

This is where you place your three recommendations and explain the options. This can be a call to action and a signpost to the steps required. Only communicate in summaries. If they need the detail, they will ask for it and you will have it available.

If you keep these three words in mind when having your meetings, you will keep the focus on what is really important. You'll see more on this later.

Key Chapter Two Takeaways

- Meet with your sponsor and get the headlines.
    - Ask the key questions, write down the

answers and get agreement.
- Do not stray from the TNA.
  - Avoid any design, development, or delivery of training.
- Find the names of the key people on the project.
  - Reach out to them, introduce yourself, and explain the purpose of the TNA.
- Build a review team.
  - Ask the sponsor for three senior people who have a good balance of business and project knowledge.
- Remember to keep the Why, What, and How in your mind.
  - Inspire people with the Why at the beginning of the TNA presentation.

Chapter 3

Use a Successful Method

"Having defined the problem, the first step towards a solution is the acquisition of data." - Roj Blake

Having a method in mind before you begin the TNA has several benefits.

- You can explain your method and get buy-in from other people
- You look and sound professional
- You have pre-determined checklists and gates to pass through so you cannot forget anything
- It focuses your thinking and time
- It challenges your assumptions

- People appreciate you are prepared

I have my own method which includes techniques and ideas that I have picked up while working for many clients. I have found it simple and useful. If you follow my template, it will force you to ask the right questions.

If you are a freelancer then you will have probably agreed a set number of days to complete the TNA. The worst situation is when you have run out of time. I know a trainer who agreed to deliver a completed TNA in nine days. He failed to do the groundwork at the beginning and dived straight into interviewing people. He asked for more time to no avail. He asked for more time and was not given it. He handed in the work he had completed so far plus his invoice, which was rejected. As the agency he used did a lot of business with the client, it took the client's side. He had wasted nine days of his time for no pay, damaged his reputation and also wasted the client's time.

I want to encourage you to download the templates from my website and walk your own way through them. Try them on for size and see how they feel. You might decide to use all of my method or just part of it. What matters is that you are aware of one way of doing it that you can fine tune to your own style.

I spoke about first steps in the previous chapter, so by this stage you should know who the major players are and be ready to ask questions and collect data. You need somewhere to put that data, and that is what we will cover in this chapter.

Action step - download the Main_TNA.docx template from www.trainersguide.com

The Main TNA Document

I use a template which I have developed over the years. It has elements that I have found useful for different clients. A lesson learnt is to ask all the questions and record the responses, even if you think the question is irrelevant. I have asked questions I thought were pointless only to find that the answer has completely changed the outcome for the TNA.

One of my clients wanted E-Learning as the solution. This should have been easy to implement in theory. I found out by asking, that the 700 delegates who needed training were not allowed to leave their desks to do the training and that their PCs were capable of running the E-Learning. Everybody had smart phones, so we produced an app that they could load up and use. The training took 20 minutes, and they were allocated this time as part of their shift pattern. One enormous benefit was that they could easily revisit the app whenever they liked, as it was on their phones.

Stick to your template and add data and findings as you go. This document is in Word and can get big. You should use it to record summary information. Excel is the right place to store the detail which will inform your TNA.

I set the Main_TNA document out into the following sections:

- Overview
    - Current Situation
    - Key Objectives
    - Initial perspective from client
    - Sequence

- Timing
  - How will you know the training has been successful?
  - Key people involved in quality assurance and sign-off
  - Outcomes if training is not completed
  - Other activities which may affect this project
  - Expectations
  - Legal or regulatory requirements
- Roles and Resources
  - Current status
  - Roles
  - Integration with the HR skills matrix
  - Out of scope requirements
  - Available resources
  - Learning Management System (LMS)
- Recommendations

Let's start with the overview section. This has many headings but shouldn't take you too long to complete after having met with the sponsor. The following is an example from a real TNA completed for a manufacturing company. I will call them Company X.

- Overview
  - In March, a project was started to create a shared service centre. This centre would run all the worldwide finance functions from one location. Additional employees would be hired and teams created to support the new service centre.

- Current Situation
  - Company X are implementing an Oracle Financials solution. The system is being customised and there are several non-standard processes. The project team have expressed concern that training has not been a feature of the project so far and urgently need to have a plan in place. A UAT (user acceptance testing) system has been created, but a training instance is not yet available.

- Key Objectives
  - To provide role-based skills and knowledge to experienced and new employees to enable

them to use Oracle Financials efficiently. This will involve process and specific task training but will not cover accountancy training.

- Initial perspective from client
  - Several managers / team leaders have expressed a preference for classroom training supported by E-Learning with process documentation as an online resource.

- Sequence
  - UAT will start in September and the plan is to go-live with the GL (general ledger), procurement and AP (accounts payable) modules in November, followed by the second go-live phase of AR (accounts receivable) in February. Training will be required for UAT and both go-live phases.

- Timing
  - UAT training must be done in August and the GL, Procurement and AP training must be no later than three weeks before go-live,

which is set for the first week in November. The second wave of training will need to be no later than three weeks before the second go-live, which is the first week in February. New employees are being hired and should be in role by September.

- How will Company X know that the training has been successful?
    - Employees will be clear about the skills required for their role and will be confident in using the Oracle system correctly.
    - Online documentation and process guides will be available at all times.
    - A legacy of training materials will be available so that classroom events can be run easily in the future as new employees are hired or existing employees change roles.
    - Employees will have been tested after their training and a record of their success will contribute to their career progression.

- Key people involved in the quality assurance sign-off

- Finance Director – initiator and final sign-off
- Project Manager – final sign-off
- GL Manager – reviewer
- Procurement Manager – reviewer
- AR Manager – reviewer

- Outcomes if training is not completed
    - If training is not delivered, then incorrect usage of the system and unnecessary mistakes will become the norm.
    - The method of training new hires is to sit 1 to 1 with them and go through the screens. This depends on the employee who is delivering the training being able to understand the processes correctly.
    - Individuals may experience high levels of stress if they are asked to use a new system with no training.

- Other activities which may affect this project
    - This project is part of a larger initiative to update and improve systems within the company. The Aquarius Project has started

> and will deliver a global supply chain system in two years time. This will use Oracle Financials for recording costs.
> - If specific requirements arise from the Aquarius Project, then this could affect the design of the Oracle Financials project. These changes would need to be reflected in the training materials. I recommend that we have a monthly update from the Aquarius team.

- Expectations
  - There are no major changes to Oracle technology in the immediate future apart from what is generated by the Aquarius Project.
  - Employees will be available in September to attend training.
  - Classrooms are available to deliver training.
  - An up-to-date training instance will be available.

- Legal or regulatory requirements
  - The leasing team must be tested and have

passed the system training before they can use the system. This is a regulatory requirement, and all test scores must be documented.

By asking the correct questions, I discovered much useful information. This project is part of a bigger one which takes precedence. This means that unexpected changes could happen. I also discovered that testing some delegates after training is essential to Company X.

At this stage, I would go back to the sponsor and run through the findings so far. Ask them if anything has been missed. Request that they drop you an email to confirm they are happy with the content so far. This is your first gate to get through. It shapes the whole of the TNA from here.

Key Chapter Three Takeaways

- Use a method
    - It will save you time and make you look professional

- Ask the right questions
  - Record all the information in the Main_TNA.docx document
- Be aware that there may be other factors in the background which could impact the TNA

Chapter 4

Interview with a Business Analyst

"I believe in evidence. I believe in observation, measurement, and reasoning, confirmed by independent observers. I'll believe anything, no matter how wild and ridiculous, if there is an evidence for it. The wilder and more ridiculous something is, however, the firmer and more solid the evidence will have to be." - Isaac Asimov

OK, we're ready to begin. I've chosen to interview the business analyst first because this person may be your best source of top quality information. Most system projects have at least one business analyst but will probably have more depending on the complexity of the project. You need to find the right people to help you, so get a list of the business analysts that details their areas of expertise. If you get this bit right, you will save yourself a massive amount of time.

Top Tip - Business analysts are generally looking forward. They are interested in the new system and the new processes and functionality. Always ask them questions about the future. The change team are the people on the project to ask about the existing system and the gaps between that and the new system.

A good business analyst will have excellent knowledge of the new system but more importantly, they will understand the big objectives of the organisation. This is crucial, as these objectives will guide the functionality of the system. Over time, you may move from the TNA phase to building and delivering the training. The business analysts will be able to pass questions from users on to you as you can answer them easily. Trust and the free flow of information are key.

I remember meeting with a business analyst. We were talking about the cash management for the organisation and I needed to create some training on how to manage bank statements in multiple currencies and regions. The individual analyst knew the software inside out. Our discussion went from the Why to the What to the How and they ended up building sample bank statement files for me and reviewing my training material. They even came to the training in case there were questions.

For me, this was the gold standard of how a business analyst should behave. Previously I mentioned you should ask your sponsor to communicate that you are doing the TNA. This gives you the authority to introduce yourself, set up a meeting, and build a relationship.

I always create a Word document template to capture the information from the interview. It might seem overkill, but it is so easy to forget the conversations you have had. I either print it and write on the printed page or type up the conversation in Word as we go along. Do not rely on your memory. You can download a suitable template from my website.

Action Step - download the Business Analyst Interview.docx document

The right words make all the difference

A business analyst is a bridge between the organisation and the programmers. Their job is to interpret the needs of the organisation and communicate it to the programmers. When this is done well, everything is documented and up to date.

One unfortunate instance occurred with a client a few years ago who paid a 'big' consultancy firm to document their processes. The job cost over a million pounds. When the material was examined closely, it contained screen shots from a completely different client. The 'big' consultancy firm had copied and pasted from a similar project. Hopefully, your documentation will be of a higher quality.

If you can talk the same language as the business analyst, then you will get a lot further in your conversation. So, here is a quick tip. Ask them about the taxonomy.

Taxonomy is the practice and science of categorisation or classification. The business analyst will use a method to capture the processes and should be able to show it to you. Typically, the processes are organised on four levels but can be over five:

- Level 1
  - Business Process Area
- Level 2
  - Business Process
- Level 3
  - Activity
- Level 4
  - Tasks

As you get lower in the hierarchy, you will see more documents. Here is an example of a real finance business process hierarchy:

- Level 1 - financial control and reporting
- Level 2 - capture transactions
- Level 3 - record and edit standard journal entries
- Level 4 - enter journal via spreadsheet

If I needed to know how to enter a journal via a spreadsheet, there should be a level 4 document explaining the steps. This is pure gold when you are creating training materials, as you can copy the steps and use them to build your materials. However, we are at the TNA stage, so we are interested in the whole hierarchy. You may find that the business analyst uses a software application that you can use to drill down through the hierarchy. Typically, I see Word documents on a SharePoint drive. Either way, this information is valuable because it can suggest your course names and groupings.

Top Tip - Level 2 will give you your course names. Level 3 will give you the sections in your courses and Level 4 will give you the specific tasks to cover in each section. We will look at tasks closely in another chapter. You can also use this in reverse. If you find a Level 4 document that describes a task, you can walk back up the hierarchy to see where it fits in to a process.

Your goal is to come out of this meeting with the full taxonomy. This provides you with a brilliant list of courses, sections, and topics defined as business processes, activities and tasks. Often on projects, the documentation is incomplete or poor. You need to make the best of what you can get. However, I have found on occasion that the Level 4s are listed as titles but have no documentation behind them. At the TNA stage, this is sufficient as we usually only need the names of the tasks.

The interview

I usually book an hour with a business analyst. The hope is that if they can provide you with the taxonomy, you can help yourself outside of the meeting and be self-sufficient. Have a template ready to record their responses:

- Name
- Date
- Process area
- How to access the taxonomy
- Key system changes that impact the client
- Key process changes that impact the client
- How is testing going?
- What are the major bugs at this stage?
- What are the key tasks belonging to the different roles?

There are quite a few questions here. Some of them are easy to answer but there are some that need unpacking:

- Key system changes that impact the organisation:
    - This could be moving from an existing system to an entirely new one from a different supplier. All the navigation and ways of working will be completely different.
- Key process changes that impact the organisation:
    - The processes could remain the same, so you just need to train on the new system. However, this is unusual as most organisations want to take advantage of the change to improve their processes. Typically, the processes will change as well as the system.
- What are the key tasks belonging to the different roles?
    - This is big. The analyst should be able to give you a role matrix which matches the business roles to the taxonomy.

Top Tip - Grab the role matrix document and don't let go.

This is another piece of gold. The role matrix gives you the business role names and what they do on the system. It is a crucial tool for you to group users against your courses.

Key Chapter Four Takeaways

- Ask the business analyst for the taxonomy
  - This is your key to the business processes and will inform you about potential course areas and names
- Ask what the system will be
  - Analysts think about the new system the whole time. Refrain from asking them about past events if possible.
- Ask the business analyst for the role matrix
  - This gives you role names and how they match to the tasks in the system

Chapter 5

Interview with a Change Manager

"Change has a bad reputation in our society. But it isn't all bad – not by any means. In fact, change is necessary in life – to keep us moving, to keep us growing, to keep us interested. Imagine life without change. It will be static, boring, dull." – Dr. Dennis O'Grady

The change manager role is focused on planning, delivering and tracking the change deliverables. Different organisations associate different tasks with this role, but generally the change manager will do the following:

- Build relationships with the user communities

- Develop and issue communications
- Ensure that the organisation is aware of the system change
- Document the impact of system and processes changes
- Identify and manage resistance from the user communities
- Support training development and delivery

A good change manager will know the company structure, the personalities and the drivers for change. They will work with the business analysts, project managers and solution architect. You can always go to a change manager to find out what is planned for the future and the problems anticipated. There will be many.

I worked with an excellent change manager recently who was interested in the entire process of the project. They produced a detailed change impact analysis document. They wanted to know about the testing and the training in detail. It was important to see what was covered in testing and training and if there were any discrepancies between the two. I had to prove that every test script was covered by a training solution. They attended the daily testing review sessions and wanted to know exactly what the testers thought of the solution and what difficulties they had. This is exactly the kind of change manager needed.

The Interview

Book an hour with the change manager. You can always book another meeting if you need to. Change managers are usually excellent communicators and enthusiastic about the idea of training. If you think about it, your training solution is going to solve many issues for them. A good training solution anticipates the organisation's issues early before they arise as a problem. Testing directly affects a small percentage of the organisation, but training will be visible to everybody who uses the system.

Top Tip - Promote your training as a powerful solution to make the change manager's life easy. Tell them that if you can get the TNA right, the training will be a dream and that it will head off the big change issues at the pass. Everybody likes a simple life and this approach will encourage them to give you the information you need and to help in other ways.

Have a template ready to record their responses:

- Name
- Date
- Background to the new system
- Key system changes that impact the client
- Key process changes that impact the client
- How to access the change impact analysis document
- What do you think is the biggest win that we could make with training?
- What is the best medium to deliver the training to the organisation?

Let me break down some of these questions and explain why you should ask them and what you really want to know.

- Key system changes that impact the client
  - You want to know the history behind how they chose the new system and what are the key changes. Organisations do not spend for

fun. They have gone through pain in order to get this far. Find out what is so much better about the new system. The change manager should know this as it is their job to sell the system to the general staff population. This information can help you focus on what is key to the organisation.

- Key process changes that impact the client
  - If the organisation just re-creates the old system with new technology, they will miss a trick. Every big implementation of new software will look at refining or changing the processes. This can have a big impact on the employees. A common trend in system implementations is to centralise admin tasks into a shared service centre. For a worldwide company, this can mean hiring a whole new team in a central location and making the admin people at country level redundant. This won't be popular with the people who are losing their jobs. The worst atmosphere I have experienced on a project was when the system was delayed by 18 months. They had

already told the employees that they were being made redundant at the first date of the go-live. They then had to beg people to stay in their jobs until the system eventually went live.

- What is the biggest win that we could make with training?
  - This really gets the change manager on your side. They want the project to go-live successfully with everybody capable of using the new system from day one. They want to avoid any shocks on day one and also to avoid support issues afterwards. This answer is obvious to both of you, but verbalising it and writing it down gets the change manager thinking about training as a solution to help them.
- What is the best medium to deliver the training to the organisation?
  - This is jumping the gun a little, but it can feed into your recommendations. You may think you know the organisation and what it likes, but the change manager can give you

extra or new information. They will know culturally what the organisation likes. Ask about classroom, E-Learning and webinars. Ask about the technology available. More about this later.

The key document you need to take from this meeting is the Change Impact Analysis document.

Change Impact Analysis Document

This is typically an Excel spreadsheet document. The change manager will add rows to this workbook as they receive input from conference room pilots, training, testing and talking to the user community. It will have columns for:

- Change - What?
- Impact - What?
- Impact - Who?
- Change Impact Analysis (CIA)
    - People
    - Process

- Systems
- Data
* Change Action Plan (CAP)

Top Tip - Pay close attention to the CAP. This is where the actions for different teams are detailed. Have a look at all the training actions. If you talk to the change manager about this, use the acronym CAP. It's a great rapport builder to use their language.

Key Chapter Five Takeaways

* Ask for the Change Impact Analysis document
  - This tells you the key gaps between the old system and the new one.
* Find out about the culture of the organisation
  - Ask why they chose the new system and how the organisation will react to it.
* Ask about how training could be a win for the project
  - This gets the change manager on your side as you will actually save them time and pain.
* Ask about the medium that the organisation prefers

for training

- If you promote E-Learning but they don't like it or use it, then you are on to a loser. Maybe, the network just won't support E-Learning. In addition there may be foreign language issues, so they may prefer written documentation that they can work through at their own speed.

- Focus on the Change Action Plan (CAP)

Chapter 6

Interview with a Test Manager and a Team Manager

"Science is not, despite how it is often portrayed, a series of absolute truths. Rather, it is a series of ideas that try to make sense of what we observe." - Brian Schmidt

You have already read about the two major interviews you must do to get the key information. There are other interviews that you should and could do. I'll include two of them here to give you some guidance. I have included templates on my website www.trainersguide.guru and I strongly recommend that you use them. Record each meeting to avoid the real risk of forgetting the details.

Test Manager

The test manager is focused on testing the new system and making sure it is fit for purpose. It is one of the most difficult jobs to do as there are a lot of resources that the testing manager is reliant on. They will probably have a team of people to create test scripts and manage the testing sessions. Typically, the people in this team will map to the business process areas (Level 1) in the taxonomy. If you are new to this way of working with systems then I can tell you that you will quickly get used to it. People identify their work with their Level 1 in the taxonomy. If you ask a question of the wrong person, then they will answer "That's more of a procurement question, please ask the relevant colleague".

Typically, the test manager will do the following:
- Plan, co-ordinate and control testing
- Develop test scripts and methodologies
- Report, track and create test reports of the outcomes

The Test Manager Interview

Book 30 minutes with the test manager. You can always book another meeting if needed. Test managers are very busy people. They are typically happy to meet you because you will solve a problem for them. The colleagues who will do the testing will need training. Testing can go on for weeks and if the testers are not trained, there will be confusion. Much of this can be avoided if training is done before testing and the testing manager knows this.

Top Tip - The sponsor and the reviewers often forget about training for the testers. This must be part of your TNA. Don't let them brush it aside or you will get caught out later on.

Have a template ready to record their responses:

- Name
- Date
- What is the scope of testing?
- What test scripts are available?
- What type of training do the testers need?

Let me break down some of these questions and explain why I am asking them and what I really want to know:

- What is the scope of testing?
  - You might assume that everything gets tested on a new system, however there will be some things that are out of scope for technical or commercial reasons. Find out what is not included.
- What test scripts are available?
  - This will give you an idea of how prepared the testing team is. Don't be fooled by a spreadsheet with a list of test script titles. Examine a few and check that detailed steps are present. Once you know which test scripts are ready and their quality, you have a good idea of how much training is required.
- What type of training do the testers need?
  - Let's assume the test scripts are good. This helps the testers out, but if they don't know how to navigate around the system, they will still struggle. Ask if they need business

process training and navigation training. Some test managers stick to the scripts, while others will link several scripts together to cover an end-to-end process. If the testers are doing this kind of testing, then they need to understand the process. Ask how many testers there will be and what training they need.

Team Manager

A team manager will be a people manager in the business. They probably won't have a direct role in the project but will be a user and will manage users of the system when it goes live.

I like to interview a few of these in the organisation, but it isn't strictly required. That is because this will probably not directly influence the facts in the TNA (such as number of users and roles) but will do the following:

- You get to extend your network in the organisation
- You find out more about the culture of the people

using the system
- You will find out how they respond to training
- You will discover issues they want to communicate

Have a template ready to record their responses:

- Name
- Date
- What is the team responsible for and how many people work in it?
- What is the best system training they have had? Why was it good?
- Would they be interested in reviewing training materials when they are being prepared?

Let me break down some of these questions and explain why I am asking them and what I really want to know:

- What is the team responsible for and how many people work in it?
    - You need to know where they fit into the taxonomy. This way of thinking will help you design the courses to match the organisation

roles. Do they use multiple business processes in the taxonomy? If so, how are you going to handle that in the TNA?

- What is the best system training they have had? Why was it good?
  - This is a loaded question that could go badly. They may tell you that their system training has been poor in the past. They may tell you about all the issues they have had with the old system. If they are negative, use this as an opportunity to describe how you think the training could be done. If they are positive, listen carefully and try to include some of their feelings in the TNA.
- Would they be interested in reviewing training materials when they are being prepared?
  - This is not strictly in the scope of the TNA, but if you get to the stage of developing materials, you will need helpful people to put some time into reviewing your materials. Take the initiative and ask.

Key Chapter Six Takeaways

- Check the scope of the testing
  - Do not include topics in your TNA if they are out of scope.
- Find out what test scripts are available and ask for access to them.
  - Have a look at the list and open a few. This will give you a good feel for the quality.
- Tell the test manager you are planning to train the testers in the TNA.
  - It would be risky to send testers in without ever having seen the new system. Make sure you get the numbers of testers and the training needed.
- Ask the team manager about the previous system training experience
  - They might give you some good ideas about how best to deliver the training.

Chapter 7

How to Transform the Taxonomy into Courses

> "Education is not a heavy load to carry, so get educated!" - Sean "The Prophet" McNicholas

You are now swimming in information. You have interviewed the key players on the project and have some great raw data. There will be an expectation in the project that you will produce something. The pressure is on! This is the stage where you can feel overwhelmed. Your task is to refine the data down to the key elements of your TNA. Discard anything that is not useful. Be ruthless about this.

Here is a recap of the key documents that you have hopefully downloaded.

Taxonomy

This is a navigable piece of software that presents the taxonomy or a series of documents on a SharePoint site. This was introduced in a previous chapter. Either way, you need to drill through the levels to get the data. The processes are organised into levels.

Top Tip - Ask the business analyst if there is a spreadsheet version. There usually is, and the advantage of this is that you can use Excel filtering to restrict the data.

The data is organised using the following levels:

- Level 1
    - Business process area
- Level 2
    - Business process
- Level 3
    - Activity
- Level 4
    - Tasks

You need to translate all this information into courses that contain topics. Let's assume that you can get the spreadsheet with all this data. The next step is to start filtering:

- Look at all the Level 1 data
    - These are high-level aspects of the system. An example from a finance system would be "Financial Control and Reporting". It's a very broad topic and will be the parent for the Level 2 processes. This could form a series of courses.
- Look at all the Level 2 data
    - These are lower-level process areas that are grouped within the parent. An example from a finance system would be "Capture Transactions". This is the level on which you will build your courses.
- Look at all the Level 3 data
    - These are lower-level activity areas that are grouped within a business process. An example from a finance system would be "Record and Edit Standard Journal Entries".

These are your chapters in the course.

- Look at all the Level 4 data
  - This is the lowest level. These are the specific instructions on how to do one task, click by click. These instructions are your best possible resource when you are creating your training material. However, don't get too close to them when building the TNA . The titles of the Level 4 data will give you the specific tasks and, therefore, the objectives of your course.

You now have your raw data about what the tasks are in the system and how they are organised. It's time to create a spreadsheet containing this data. You can probably copy from the spreadsheet that the business analyst gave you. You don't need all the columns. Start with these four:

- Business process area
- Business process
- Activity
- Task

You then need to add four more columns:

- Course
- Score 1
- Score 2
- Duration (leave blank for now)

This is a big step. You need to identify for each task, which course it will be in. You can get the names of the courses from the Level 2 business process. The fifth column is the course name and in Excel you can change this as you need to. You don't always want it to be the same name as the Level 2 process. If you do this for each task, you can use Excel filtering to look at one course at a time.

Score 1 and Score 2

This is a significant win for you. These two columns raise you above the normal training consultant. You need to understand this perfectly and be able to explain it to others. These two columns have no data at this stage but will contain a score for two metrics about each task. Fear not, as you can download a template (TNA Workbook.xlsm) from my website to get you going.

The idea is that you score every task out of three using the two columns. You will decide what the criteria are, but the outcome is that you have a method of working out which topics must be covered in training and which can be a lower priority. A score of 1 is low and a score of 3 is high. I like to use two criteria:

- What is the impact on the day-to-day business?
- How many people will carry out this task?

You need to go back to the business analyst to work through all the tasks. This sounds complicated, but I have found that it is easy for them to score each topic. You are doing this so that you can produce a nine box matrix. You will end up with a dual score for each task. If a task scored 1,1 then you know the impact is low and the number of people using that task is tiny. An example would be setting up the dates for financial periods. This is probably done once every five years by one person. They will know how to do it without training, so it is a low priority. At the other end of the spectrum, you could have a task to enter expenses on the system. Everybody does this and the impact is big if people are not trained. This would get a score of 3,3.

Imagine a nine box matrix. The bottom left is 1,1 and the top right is 3,3. All the tasks will fit into one of the nine boxes depending on the combination of the two scores. When you are presenting your recommendations, you can explain exactly how many tasks will be covered in training and why you are excluding some of them.

I like to think of this as an inverted 'L' shape. We always want to train the outside inverted 'L' shape of the nine box grid. If we have time and the resources we would include the next level inverted 'L'. That leaves our last box 1,1 which we are unlikely to train out. This is a brilliant way of communicating what could be trained and what we need to focus on.

Luckily, I have already built this in Excel for you. You can download it from my site, paste in your own tasks and build the scoring. The spreadsheet builds a diagram of the nine box grid and this reacts immediately to any data changes you make. I also include an extra column to identify if a training solution has been created for the task. This isn't useful at the

TNA stage, but is essential once you build your training material.

Additional Tasks and Courses

The business analysts will always focus on the system tasks. They may not be interested in the problems of people using the system. You will definitely have to add extra courses that will help the users beyond the system tasks, such as:

- General navigation
    - How to find your way around the system
- How to run reports
    - On most systems, there will be more than one way to run reports
- Master data management
    - An overview of how the data is organised and how it differs from the old system
- Approvals
    - Depending on the complexity of the system, you may need to explain the responsibilities and methods of managing approvals

You will need to define the specific tasks within each course and add these to the spreadsheet with their own course name and scores. Each course will have multiple tasks.

Top Tip - Use Excel to filter on a course name and this lists all the tasks. These become the objectives in your course descriptions.

Course Names

I have suggested that the course names come from the Level 2 titles in the taxonomy. This is a great start and if you keep the names consistent, it will help communicate the ideas for your training to other people in the business. However, the names have come from the business analysts and they probably got them from the supplier of the software. This may be fine, but do look closely at the names and change them to suit the organisation. The delegates benefit from clear communication.

Course Timings

This is where you will have to use your experience of delivering training to estimate the course durations. You will need to think about whether this is a pure E-Learning solution or a classroom type event or a mixture. You may have to provide different timings for each scenario. I work off how long I think a classroom event would take and use that as a guide. For instance, a course training people to create financial journals could take four hours if you include explanations, demonstrations, practice sessions and breaks. I use minutes rather than hours. Don't worry about this being completely accurate. Make an estimate and be generous as you can always adjust it later.

Key Chapter Seven Takeaways

- Look closely at the taxonomy.
  - Create your own spreadsheet and add all the tasks. Score each one with the help of the business analyst
- Enter course names which you get from the Level 2

names in the taxonomy and associate them with the tasks

- You can always update the course names when you refine your recommendations.

Chapter 8

Courses, Roles and Delegates

"An investment in knowledge pays the best interest."
- Benjamin Franklin

We are now getting to the nitty gritty as there is now a list of course names with tasks. The next thing to do is to work on the roles matrix.

The outcome from this work is that you will have your course titles and the names of the people who need to attend. However, at this stage, you shouldn't be too worried about the names of the individuals. What you are really after is the number of delegates per course.

Roles Matrix

The role matrix is typically an Excel spreadsheet, which has two important columns:

- Organisation role - a role name that the organisation will recognise such as finance manager
- System role - a software role that enables functionality in the system

In reality, the business analyst will have many more columns, but you are only interested in these two. An organisation role may have many system roles. When a user logs in, their profile will already have system roles associated with them. This determines what they can do in the system. This is key information when you are describing the courses in your TNA.

Top Tip - Think back to the taxonomy and the processes. The role matrix describes the job roles in the organisation and the level of their responsibility in the system. This is all linked to the taxonomy. You should now get a feel for how the system has been designed.

The organisation roles are the roles that you associate with your courses. The average user will have no visibility of system roles but should know their organisation role. Each course must link to one or more organisation roles so we know who to send on the courses.

Create a new worksheet in your workbook and copy the organisation role titles as columns from the role matrix. You can now add in rows for courses and enter the course names in the first column. Whenever a course is related to a business role, enter the course name in the cell. You now have a matrix of all your courses and how they relate to the organisation roles. You will find a tab in the TNA Workbook.xlsm spreadsheet which I introduced you to in the last chapter.

This is important because this helps you visualise the impact of certain courses. Think about the tasks that everybody in the company does. An example would be navigating around the system. Everybody needs training and so every organisation role will have a 'Y' against the navigation course. It also highlights where there are gaps you need to investigate.

Delegates

The role manager will provide you with a list of the users for the new system. This list will have been worked on for a long time. It has wide-reaching consequences across the entire project for licensing and resources and so it must be correct. Whoever carries out this task has a serious job. If they get it wrong, people could be creating a purchase order, adding a supplier invoice in their own name and paying it to themselves and creating a massive fraud! In the film "Monty Python and the Holy Grail" there was a character called the Black Knight. His big quote was "None Shall Pass" and that is the required approach for that job.

The role manager is making the segregation of duties safe for the organisation. They should be able to give you all the names with all the roles. They might tell you it is confidential company information. Escalate it if you need to. In the future, when you get to the scheduling and delivery phase, you will need these names. If they really insist it is an issue, ask them to blank the names out. All you really need to know is the number of people in the roles. This is liable to change as people join and leave the company, but it is good enough to give the number of employees per role.

You need to add another sheet into your workbook. Use the copy function and copy all the delegate and role data from the user list spreadsheet. You will now have a matrix with a 'Y' where a user is in a role.

Top Tip - The role matrix is pure gold for your TNA as it gives you the numbers of people per role. You can associate the roles to the courses and you will have your facts about how many people need training. You can easily create summaries to find out how many users are in each role. A delegate can carry out multiple roles each which could be associated with a particular course. This could result in a single delegate being counted more than once as a candidate for training on the same course. This simple error will make your summaries incorrect. The workbook I supply contains a macro to do this correctly.

Excel Skills

Not everybody is an expert on Excel. If you are a freelancer and feel exposed, go outside the organisation for help. I have an extensive network of people I can call on for help. I use www.fiverr.com to find expert assistance such as the creation of an Excel workbook to your specification. If you go outside the company, make sure that you do not share company data. You could create some fake sample data for whoever is going to build your spreadsheet and then paste in the real data later.

Make sure you do not share data. This is a shortcut to getting fired and possibly sued!

Please have a look at my website www.trainersguide.guru. I have included examples of every document I have mentioned, so download them and have a look and then paste in your own data. Even if you find these templates don't quite fit your organisation, you have a significant starting point.

Key Chapter Eight Takeaways

- Look closely at the taxonomy for the project.

- Create your own spreadsheet and add all the tasks. Score each one with the help of the business analyst
- Enter course names which you get from the Level 2 names in the taxonomy and associate them with the tasks
    - You can always update the course names when you refine your recommendations
- Enter the organisation role and system role names into your spreadsheet
    - The organisation role names are the ones that will be used in your TNA

Chapter 9

How to Summarise your Findings

"Take nothing on its looks; take everything on evidence. There's no better rule." - Charles Dickens

It's time again to catch your breath. You have interviewed people, gathered data and created your own spreadsheet. Now is the time to put it all together.

Events So Far

Let's have a look at the sequence of events that have got you this far.

1. Met with the sponsor and agreed the requirement

- You asked the key questions, made notes and got confirmation
2. Met with the business analyst and got the taxonomy
    - You distilled this information into a spreadsheet and added customised course names
3. Met with the change manager and got the change impact analysis
    - You picked out the key changes and the CAP
4. Met with the test manager and team managers and got the test scripts
    - You found out what is in and out of scope and who needs training for user acceptance testing

The next task is to take the information from your spreadsheet and to summarise it.

Delegates' Worksheet

This worksheet contains a row for each delegate and a column for each organisation role. Place a "Y" in each cell where a delegate is a member of a role. A summary is automatically calculated for you, so you have a count of the delegates in each role.

Roles and Courses

This worksheet contains a column for each course and a row for each organisation role. The course code is entered in a cell if it is associated with a course. A summary of the number of delegates for each course is automatically calculated.

Courses and Tasks

The Tasks Worksheet contains course titles (which you got from the L2 processes) and the tasks within each course. I like to filter this information by course and then place it in a separate Word document for each course.

You can download an example from my website called Course Description - General Ledger - Capture Transactions.docx. Here is an example of the headings and type of information to include:

- Course Title
  - General Ledger - Capture Transactions
- Course Description
  - This course will cover entering and inquiring on standard and sub-ledger journals, completing account inquiries and approving and posting journals.
- Course Objectives - You will be able to:
  - Create and inquire on different types of journal
  - Complete an account inquiry and drill down
  - Create a manual journal
  - Create a journal via a spreadsheet
- Duration
  - 240 minutes
- Prerequisites
  - Navigation course
- Target Audience
  - General Ledger agent
  - General Ledger manager

You need to be careful about scope creep. You don't need to go into a lot of detail here, as that will be done at the design stage. The key things we need are the audience and the length of time. The duration is an estimate at this stage as you haven't decided whether this is classroom, E-Learning, self reading or a mixture. I tend to be generous as you can always refine it later if challenged.

Do this for all the courses you have identified on the spreadsheet. It shouldn't take long as you can copy and paste much of the information and if you are skilled on Excel, you could build a macro to create the Word documents for you from one key stroke.

Enter the duration for each course in the Roles and Courses worksheet.

Edit the Main TNA Document

Now is the time to go back to the Main TNA document and to complete the remaining sections. Here are the headings with some sample text as a guide.

- Current status
    - There is a wide spectrum of employee skills

and knowledge, which is caused by the volume of recruitment this year. Some employees have used Oracle in other companies. Employees hired into roles already have the required accountancy or admin training, but we will provide a complete Oracle training solution so that each role is fully supported.

- Roles
  - Provide a table with the list of roles and the number of delegates.
- Integration with the HR skills matrix
  - Currently, technology training is not directly linked to career progression. The HR team is looking at including Oracle skills in the skills matrix they maintain for the finance roles. If they decide to do this, then they will need to decide whether attendance at training is enough or specific testing is required to prove attainment of a skill.
- Out of scope requirements
  - The initial go-live releases will include standard reports. Soon, there will be a new

reporting solution which will allow certain job roles to create their own reports. This technology has not been decided on yet. A new role of reporting manger will be created once the reporting technology has been defined.

- Available resources
  - Process guides exist, but this does not extend to all the level 4 documents. Standard Operating Procedures (SOPs) exist for about 20% of the processes.
- Learning management system
  - Company X have a good LMS which we can use to host the course descriptions and learning paths. The Company X LMS can create custom invitations, record attendance, evaluate performance, and provide reports.

Task Analysis

Add a screenshot of the nine box matrix. This gives you a

count of the tasks that need to be trained and a ranking in the nine boxes to identify its importance. You may need to explain the concept of tasks from the taxonomy. Once people understand that, they love the picture of the summary information. It gives them great insight into the analysis you have done.

If people want to see the data and query the scores, you can show them the tab with the data on, but don't get drawn into editing this immediately. Stick to the facts and show them you know what needs covering in the courses and that you have identified some tasks which are a low priority.

Courses and Delegates

Review the Delegates worksheet on your workbook. Every delegate will have a row and the organisation roles will be in columns. The role columns will also display a total number for each role. These count up the number of delegates who have a 'Y' in their cells for that role.

Create a table in the Main TNA Document with a list of the roles and the number of delegates per role. Create another table in the document with the following columns:

- Course

- Number of delegates
- Duration

This is a snapshot that is easy for the audience to understand. Don't get drawn in yet over how the training will be delivered. You will cover this in a later section.

Key Chapter Eight Takeaways

- Use Excel to capture your data and to produce the counts of delegates per course
- Use the task matrix to prioritise all of the training tasks
- Put your summaries and findings in the Main TNA document

Chapter 10

What do People Really Think about TNAs?

> "Our opinions do not really blossom into fruition until we have expressed them to someone else." - Mark Twain

I thought it would be useful to interview people whose opinion I respect on aspects of TNAs. One of the individuals is involved in the training world and may therefore be likely to think that a TNA is a good thing. The others may approach this from a different perspective outside the training bubble. I think that if you want to raise your game and become a real asset to an organisation, you need to understand the big picture.

I know these people well. I've worked with them and we've kept in touch. Knowing good people when you meet them in business and maintaining your network is your best long-term asset.

Top Tip - Build your network. Do a favour for people and they will remember it ten years later. I've had calls from people who I helped and they ring me about a piece of work they can offer me or they just want to ask for advice. Throw a pebble in the lake and watch the ripples bounce back on you, years later.

Tom Sewell - Co-Founder - Charlton House Professional Services

Tom is an entrepreneur who has co-founded an international training consultancy specialising in digital adoption services. He is a very smart guy who has an open mind and loves new ideas.

What are your expectations when you commission a TNA?

I want to understand if the training is going to deliver the outcome that the client is interested in. Training is often thought of in the context of a moment in time and I think that it should be an on-going concern that delivers value for the client throughout the lifecycle of the system/processes it's underpinning. There has to be a continuation of value beyond the original training delivery.

What are the three most important things for the TNA to clarify?

I am not interested in a TNA that is too 'lite touch'. I like to see it following a more widely recognised taxonomy and that there is rigour involved.

It should include an understanding of what the ultimate end knowledge transfer goal is, role by role. I need to be able to track back from the desired outcome, to the analysis and to the original conversation with the client. That thread should be easy to follow.

Delivery mechanisms have to be clear and I need to know how many delegates are associated with each delivery type and there needs to be a way to track all of that day-to-day from concept through to delivery.

How much detail do you like to see in a TNA?

I like it to be in a spreadsheet format. I like a universally recognised taxonomy where I can track through verticals in an ERP (Enterprise Resource Planning) or CRM (Customer Relationship Management) implementation. I need to be able to view the different lenses on the TNA, by role, territory, process, platform and others. This is only possible with high degrees of detail.

What are you looking for when you review a TNA and sign it off?

The more detail the better. It gives me confidence in the process. I am looking for a high degree of detail and for it to be easily manipulatable.

What is your best experience of a TNA?

The best experience was in the UK where the training director produced a very thorough and complete TNA that gave me the assurance that we were in a strong position.

What is your worst experience of a TNA?

I was asked last minute to help in the rollout of a big system in Asia. I was tasked with doing a QA (Quality Assurance) on the training approach and plan. The TNA hardly existed and we had just three months before go-live to try and put together a complete solution.

Matt Okesola - Change Strategist - Nterprise Ltd

Matt and I worked together for a large software company. He is always polite but asks just the right questions and knows exactly where to focus.

What are your expectations of a good TNA?

It must capture needs in the most generous way possible. People's needs start from where they are now. Capture a wide stakeholder grouping, including the end users. Context is everything, and it's about knowing what will work best.

I want people to be emotionally connected with the new project. If we involve them from the beginning, we have a higher chance they will feel connected and involved.

What can the change team offer to the training

consultant?

We can help with context! We can help you avoid missing important groups. The business as usual (BAU) is the largest audience. These people are working in the 'now' with the tools they have. You need to make sure that you see the gaps identified by business change. Feedback is gold.

Business Change can possibly offer a training lead/stream real stakeholder insight into the impacts that training would be looking to mitigate.

What does a good TNA look like?

It must capture content that is useful for all the other work streams. This gives us insight we might not have had, which is useful not only for change. A TNA should convey the approach to training without actually doing the training plan. It is a living document and should be up to date. It should build confidence that it is relevant.

What is your best experience of a TNA?

A TNA that included what happens next after go-live. It stated the training need after the go-live training is delivered. It also planned the use of a sand pit environment for use after the training. Planned updates to the training material after bugs are fixed and processes changed.

What is your worst experience of a TNA?

Promises that I had made to the organisation were not met by the TNA, and I was furious. The TNA was divorced from the training plan.

Dr Anthony Cairns - CEO - QASTM (Quality Assured Software & Testing Management)

Dr Cairns is one of the most generous people I know. He is a high achiever but does not hesitate to lend a hand.

What value do you see in a TNA?

It gives you an understanding and clarity around the depth and awareness of the training scope and how it could be applied in the organisation.

As a test manager, how can a good TNA help you in your job?

You want to use the information that has been provided on the scope and coverage to make sure that the testing meets the needs of the business. Testing and training can be closely linked.

How can the testing team help the training team during TNA design?

If you take the detailed end-to-end test scenarios which comprise many scripts, these map to the end-to-end business process. These should build the training. We can quality check between testing and training to make sure nothing is missed.

Should training cover every single thing that is tested?

In testing, you cannot test every combination. It's the same in training. You cannot train every single variation.

What level of training do you think testers from the business need?

It is very beneficial for business testers to get training first, before the testing begins. This needs to relate directly to what they will be testing and also how to do the testing.

Have you seen any examples where training didn't help?

When training has been delivered too early and also where

the users were trained on processes that they didn't actually test. A good TNA would have avoided this.

Andrew Shipley - Finance Director - Aveva

Andrew has decades of experience working at a very high level in finance. He is currently the finance integration lead at Aveva.

What are your expectations when you commission a TNA?

I expect a TNA to be diligently completed and accurately reflect the requirements of the targeted audience. I expect the person performing the TNA to have in-depth subject matter knowledge and also an understanding of the audience, to be able to properly assess the training need and ensure the audience receive the right training.

I would expect the person performing the TNA to know the business operating model and associated roles and responsibilities. Ideally, we'd have pre-defined business roles and an established training library, which standardises the TNA, and makes it consistent for people performing similar business roles.

What are the three most important things for the TNA to clarify?

It is important to understand the future role of the audience, and confirm this with the appropriate leaders to avoid any misunderstandings or mistakes. The assigner needs to clarify any specific nuances, or localisations, which might require an established training approach and materials to be adapted.

For example, where English is not the natural language of the audience to be trained. The existing knowledge of the audience should be clarified, along with their level of current expertise, which might also require the TNA to be adapted.

How much detail do you like to see in a TNA?

The level of detail depends on the maturity of the project/programme. If the business operating model, and associated business roles, are largely already defined, and standardised, and associated training materials already available, then the TNA can simply summarise the training allocation to individuals (based on their roles). However, where this is not the case, the TNA would have to detail the activities being performed and how these would be satisfied by training.

What are you looking for when you review a TNA and sign it off?

I am primarily looking for completeness and accuracy. I want every relevant person to be included and the TNA to accurately reflect their requirements. I want consistency of approach, and standards, so that people receive the same high level of training. I want to see specific consideration of the local circumstances and any factors which might impact the training approach.

What is your best experience of a TNA?

The programmes I have worked on which have gone very well have been properly resourced and organised, with dedicated training expertise. The project has a well-defined (and achievable) plan, with everyone working collaboratively to ensure deliverables and milestones are achieved on time. The audience mapping and role assignment is performed early, allowing the TNA to be executed properly and to plan. The TNA is then regularly refined and refreshed to keep it up to date.

What is your worst experience of a TNA?

When programmes are not well organised and resourced, then they usually go badly. If you don't know your audience; or what you're aiming to achieve with them; or don't allow sufficient time to perform the TNA, then this will compromise it and cause poor business readiness and bad employee experience. We might have a great new product/solution, but no one is able to use it!

Chapter 11

How to Present your TNA

"If you can't explain it simply, you don't understand it well enough." – Albert Einstein

You are now at the stage where all the work is coming to a pinnacle. You need to sell your TNA. It doesn't matter if you are an employee in an organisation or a freelancer. Your job is to get across your findings. It's up to the organisation to choose to accept these recommendations. However, they cannot reject your facts if you have done your work honestly.

There is something about this point in the process that I love. In my teens, I did Karate training and I gained my black belt at 19. In competitions, it was just me, on my own, standing up, facing my opponent. You never knew who you were going to fight. That moment when you are called up is electric. I get a real buzz out of doing my preparation, building the TNA and presenting it. It's a different challenge, but the same feeling.

When I was doing Karate, I felt I was prepared. At 19, I was fit and strong, and I had an excellent technique. I like to have that feeling when I prepare a TNA. I always have my evidence and recommendations. It doesn't matter who comes to the presentation as I am ready to answer anybody's questions.

By this stage, you will have had the TNA reviewed several times. There should be no gaping holes or mistakes. It should be solid and backed up with data. You do, however, need to think about how to get this information across to the right people. Your sponsor and review team are on your side. They have reviewed the TNA and are there to back you up.

Think about what outcome you want from this meeting. Does a decision need to come out of this meeting or is this the starting point for further discussion? Knowing this in advance can change how you do your presentation. Get guidance from your sponsor in advance.

Top Tip - make sure you know who is involved in signing off the TNA. You should have this detailed in the Main TNA document. It's worth finding out if anybody else has a significant influence on this.

I've usually been asked to present my TNA at meetings. This might be a one-off occasion or a slot in a regular meeting. I highly recommend that you find out in advance what format this meeting will take and who is attending. If you know the individuals concerned, you may prepare answers for the questions they will ask.

Think Big

It is likely that you won't get much time to present your TNA. The venue might be a meeting room or a Teams/Zoom call. Your presentation should match the time you have. I always build a PowerPoint presentation. This is an easy medium to use as you can include images and present it in a meeting room or online, but you can also email it if required.

Top Tip - Do not distribute the PowerPoint before the meeting beyond the review team. People can have a copy afterwards if needed, but give nothing away before the event.

Your focus should be on the headlines here so think big. If questions come up, then you have your spreadsheet. People like facts, they like the big numbers, they like recommendations and finally they like to make decisions. Keep this in mind as you build your presentation.

As an example, you will know the number of delegates for each course so divide this number by the maximum number of delegates you allow for each event. A course with 62 delegates would mean that you need to run eight events to cater to all the delegates. If you know the duration of the course, then you know how many trainer days this will take to deliver. Don't get too concerned about scheduling at this stage, just produce easy-to-understand summaries.

Don't underestimate the need to give basic explanations. Be obvious if you need to be. It's important for you to get your point across. Not everybody in the room will know about the project in detail or the latest training terminology.

Use the life of the project so far as part of the story. Taking 60 seconds at the beginning to set the scene switches people on to the idea and where you are in the process. Human beings respond to stories. Our brains are just designed that way.

Don't put the whole TNA on your slides. The slides should not be read out loud. They are a summary. Your job is to explain what the summary means and answer questions about how you got the data.

The Main TNA document is where all the proof and background should remain.

Your Slide Pack

I always like to start with an agenda slide. This helps people understand what is coming but also should stop questions before the right section. Here is an example:

- Overview

- Current situation
  - Key objectives
  - Sequence and timing
  - Outcomes
  - Assumptions
- Roles and Resources
  - Roles and their integration with the roles matrix
  - Available resources
  - Learning management system
  - Task analysis
  - Courses
- Conclusion
  - Recommended approach
  - Required resources
  - Timelines
  - Big picture recommendations

You can lift much of this information from the Main TNA document. Just copy and paste the information.

Timeline

Include a slide with a simple timeline. This should include the training development time, user acceptance training and training for go-live. The key takeaway from this is that you have thought about the waves of training that you are preparing for. A visual representation of the time required for each task focuses attention so do take this opportunity to invite questions.

Big Picture Recommendations

This is where I suggest you offer three recommendations. It is essential that you give the organisation a chance to compare alternatives. The three alternatives can be driven by cost, timing, technology, method, or any other considerations that affect the organisation.

Get an understanding from the interviewees as to what is appropriate for the situation. I can't easily guide you because every situation is different, but remember that the underlying facts do not change. The roles, courses and delegates remain constant. The recommendations you make are your solutions to their needs.

Example Scenario:

You have found that 600 delegates need training across 12 separate roles. You have identified 19 different courses.

First recommendation - Instructor led Training

Three training developers are required over a two-month period to create the material, followed by 80 classroom sessions delivered over a three-week period. The trainers will deliver informal training to the testers over three days.

Second recommendation

End user procurement, expenses and timesheet training will be delivered using E-Learning only, which will be created off-shore. The E-Learning will be story boarded by a seconded employee from the business. Two training consultants will create the remaining classroom material and deliver the professional user training to one hundred and 20 delegates over a two-week period.

Third recommendation

Two training consultants will create E-Learning for all

courses. These courses will be role based and all delegates will be invited via the learning management system (LMS) to attend training over a three-week period.

Doing More

I knew a physiotherapist and it fascinated me to find out how they were so successful with their treatments. I asked if I could observe a session and model what happened. Sitting alongside, I watched, made notes and asked questions afterwards. I noticed that they placed a thin blanket over the client before the treatment began. I asked why that was done as the room wasn't cold and the client was fully clothed. I was told that putting on an extra layer was adding comfort and that this unconsciously created a trusting relationship for the treatment. It really made me think how I could add more to my clients. How would this impact the relationship? I did this in my day-to-day work and really noticed a difference. If I teach a course and explain something complicated, I always make sure I have additional material to back it up if needed.

When I do a TNA, I try to give substance to my recommendations. If I suggest using an LMS in a certain way, I provide examples of how it could be done. I try to pre-empt questions and plan resources to hand out in response. Doing more is a way of thinking and behaving. Always be thinking about how you can add extra content or how you can challenge the organisation to do more or get more from this opportunity. They will love you for it because you are making a difference.

Epilogue

"Things won are done; joy's soul lies in the doing."- William Shakespeare

Firstly, I must congratulate you on finishing this book. Most people start books and never finish them. You made it, so thanks for coming along for the ride.

The next thing I want to do is tell you to test my method. Download the template files and start using them. I highly recommend you use all of them and then decide how you can change and improve them. If you have some ideas, please contact me and if they are good, I will update the templates.

I also want to suggest that you try to explain the method to a sympathetic colleague and see if it makes sense. Explaining things out loud has an amazing effect on our subconscious. I often find that the penny drops for me as I am explaining something to someone else.

If this is the first time you are doing a TNA, then you will find your own method. This book gives you a great approach and a set of templates to get you going that I know will work. You will find your own way of doing it that suits your style. You will quickly get an instinct for what is required and who to ask and how to record the information.

I have found that over the years, people remember a piece of work that I did for them and ask me to come back and do more. They are confident that I have a method and that I will produce the goods. It doesn't really matter what the field of work is, if you have a method and consistently deliver, then people will want to work with you. You may also find that people who you haven't even met recommend you and refer to you as a trusted source.

If you follow the steps and successfully deliver a TNA, then wonderful things can happen. Delegates receive the right training at the right time. They are calm and prepared on the day of go-live. The organisation will be pleased that the level of engagement and satisfaction is high. The sponsor will feel good about choosing you to do the TNA. You made something hard look easy.

Thank you so much for letting me guide you.

If you have questions, or just want to reach out, then please contact me at torrit@me.com

If you have a moment it would be appreciated if you could please leave a review on Amazon.

Good luck with everything.

Tom Mcguire

Printed in Great Britain
by Amazon